VERTEX

INTERNATIONAL PRIVATE BRAND
DESIGN COMPETITION

EDITED BY:

CHRISTOPHER DURHAM,
PRESIDENT, MY PRIVATE BRAND

PHILLIP RUSSO,
PUBLISHER, GLOBAL RETAIL BRANDS

folio28

CHARLOTTE, NORTH CAROLINA

Volume V: Vertex Awards International Retail Brand Design Competition

Published by Folio28 LLC, Charlotte, NC
www.folio28.com
www.mypbrand.com
ISBN 978-0-9915220-8-8
First Edition

TABLE OF CONTENTS

BEST OF SHOW Uniquely J Badass Espresso _____ 2

PUBLISHERS CHOICE Peaceful Piranha _____ 4

GOLD

Uniquely J Single Serve Coffee _____ 8
Uniquely J Peruvian Ground Coffee __ 10
Uniquely J Food Storage _____ 12
Uniquely J _____ 14
Fruitmojis _____ 16
Sensations by Compliments Cold Brew _ 18
El Corte Inglés Bio _____ 20
El Corte Inglés Tex Mex _____ 22
El Corte Inglés Snacks _____ 24
El Corte Inglés Beers _____ 26
GustarVita _____ 28
G'Day _____ 30
Fresh Thyme Fresh Pizza _____ 32
Presto! _____ 34
Brookshire's Seasonings _____ 36
Live Better _____ 38
Jumbo Batteries _____ 40
Albert Heijn Smoked Sausage _____ 42
Albert Heijn Cooking & Dining _____ 44
Xavier _____ 46
Monoprix Food to Go _____ 48
Jumbo Wood Oven Pizza's _____ 50
Jumbo Ice cream Lovers _____ 52
Jumbo Spices _____ 54
Woolworths Clean _____ 56
ALDI Runik _____ 58

SILVER

Uniquely J Fig & Thyme Mini Crisps __ 62
Prince & Spring Pretzel Bites _____ 64
Great Value Ice Cream Cones _____ 66
Aliada _____ 68
El Corte Inglés Gazpacho _____ 70
El Corte Inglés Panettone _____ 72
Culinary Tours _____ 74
Limited Time Originals – Holiday _____ 76
Back To College 2017 _____ 78
Market District Coffee _____ 80
Fresh Direct Just Nut Bars _____ 82
Simply Me Beauty _____ 84
7-Select GO!Smart Cold Pressed Juice _ 86
Natural Goodness _____ 88
AquaBliss Personal Care _____ 90
Prince & Spring Coconut Water _____ 92
Jumbo Fresh Juices _____ 94
Leaps & Bounds Toys _____ 96
Paderno _____ 98
Irresistibles Smoothie Mix _____ 100
Irresistibles Glow in the Dark Tissue __ 102
Woolworths Gold _____ 104
Member's Mark Organic Milk _____ 106
Consum Jam _____ 108

BRONZE

Macro _____ 112
Uniquely J Avocado Oil _____ 114
Uniquely J Cleaner _____ 116
Sam's Choice Italia _____ 118
Sam's Choice Coffee _____ 120
Prince & Spring Epsom Salts _____ 122
Earth Fare Seltzer Water _____ 124
Giant/Stop & Shop Pasta Sauce _____ 126
Etos Face Mask _____ 128
Personnelle Depilatory _____ 130
Club del Gourmet Cured Fish _____ 132
Fresh Thyme Tasty Tykes _____ 134
Fresh Thyme Freeze Dried Fruit _____ 136
Nice! _____ 138
HT Traders Granola _____ 140
7-Select GO!Yum Cold Brew Coffee __ 142
Natural Grocers _____ 144
Wellsley Farms Spices _____ 146
PNP Tiny Tots _____ 148
Live Well _____ 150
Pick Local _____ 152
Pingo Doce Pasta _____ 154
Pams Finest _____ 156
Fairway Market Grass-Fed Milks _____ 158

5 years ago, we could never have imagined the impact that the Vertex Awards would have on private brands globally. This year's record-setting class of entrants is evidence of not only Vertex's impact on design but strategy. We have pushed retailers, agencies and manufacturers to explore the boundaries of private brand, to move beyond the expected and create brands and package design that genuinely differentiate. As a celebration of the anniversary, all winners will receive a special edition artisan designed and crafted trophy.

This year's competition included more than 400 entries from 27 countries and 49 retailers. You will discover outstanding design from all around the world. Retailers are playing to win and creating compelling customer-focused brands.

We would like to thank our esteemed panel of design experts from around the world who took their charge to heart and devoted their time and energy to selecting the best of the best: Paco Adin, Rick Barrack, Danielle Beal, Paula Bunny, Linda Casey, Don Childs, Maria Dubuc, Steven Cox, Charlene Codner, Michael Duffy, Guillermo Dufranc, Masanori Eto, John Kalkowski, Loe Limpens, Fred Richards, Nick Vaus, David Ziegler-Voll and ZHOU Wenjun.

Qualifying designs must have been introduced in-store between November 2016 and November 2017. Judges scored each entry on five criteria: design, Information architecture, originality, structure, and x-factor. An overall numeric score was then assigned to each entry. Gold, Silver and Bronze Awards were awarded based on the numeric score, as a result, there are some multiple winners at a given level.

The scoring system was developed to reward the best Private Brand package design in the world, not mediocrity. To protect the integrity of the process, judges were not allowed to vote on work by their own agency. All voting was done online and votes were collected and tabulated independently, by VOCCII. This competition has been a labor of love. We know you will find inspiration in the winners and we hope to see your entry next year.

Christopher Durham
Founder, My Private Brand

Phillip Russo
Publisher, Global Retail Brands

UNIQUELY J
BADASS ESPRESSO

BEST OF SHOW

Retailer: Jet.com
Country: United States of America
Category: G3. Packaged Goods
Agency: Elmwood
Credits:
Creative Director: Laura Kind

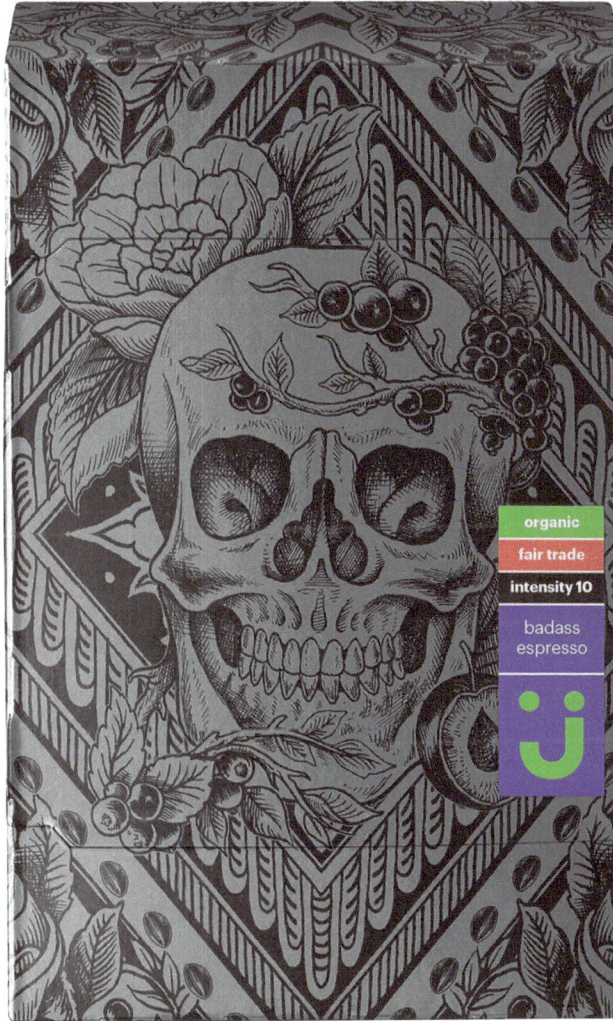

organic
fair trade
intensity 10
badass espresso

PEACEFUL PIRANHA

PUBLISHER'S CHOICE

Retailer:Hy-Vee

Country: United States of America

Category: B1. New Brand

Agency: Meyocks

Credits:

The Hy-Vee – Meyocks
Package Design Team

PEACEFUL PIRANHA™ SNACKS

PER 4 CUPS
150 CALORIES
1g SAT FAT
115mg SODIUM
0g TOTAL SUGARS

LIGHT
EXTRA VIRGIN OLIVE OIL POPC
with Himalayan Salt
NET WT 4.4 OZ (125 g)

PEACEFUL PIRANHA™ SNACKS

PER 1/2 CUP
120 CALORIES
3.5 SAT FAT
150mg SODIUM
15g TOTAL SUGARS

ITE CHOCOLATE
ED POPCORN
T 8 OZ (227 g)

PEACEFUL PIRANHA SNACKS

230 CALORIES

Double Dipped
MILK CHOCOLATE
PEANUTS
NET WT 10 OZ (283 g)

GOLD

UNIQUELY J SINGLE SERVE COFFEE

Retailer: Jet.com
Country: United States of America
Category: G3. Packaged Goods
Agency: Elmwood
Credits:
Creative Director: Laura Kind

organic
fair trade
dark roast

french roast
coffee
single serve

UNIQUELY J
PERUVIAN
GROUND COFFEE

Retailer: Jet.com
Country: United States of America
Category: G3. Packaged Goods
Agency: Elmwood
Credits:
Creative Director: Laura Kind

organic
fair trade
medium roast

peruvian
coffee
ground

NET WT 16 OZ. (453 g)

UNIQUELY J
FOOD STORAGE

Brand: Uniquely J
Retailer:Jet.com
Country: United States of America
Category: G3. Packaged Goods
Agency: Elmwood
Credits:
Creative Director: Laura Kind

double seal portion control bags

100 count, 3 1/2 IN X 5 7/8 IN (8.9 cm x 14.9 cm)

slider gallon freezer bags

50 count, 3.78L • 10 9/16 IN X 11 IN (26.8 cm x 27.9 cm)

UNIQUELY J

Retailer: Jet.com
Country: United States of America
Category: B1. New Brand
Agency: Elmwood
Credits:
Creative Director: Laura Kind

FRUITMOJIS

Retailer: Boxed

Country: United States of America

Category: G3. Packaged Goods

Agency: Prince & Spring

Credits:

Jeff Gamsey: VP of Private Brands

Chris Cheung: Creative Director

Vera Atamian: Senior Designer

Annslee DeLuca: Brand Manager & Copy Writer

Brandon Wehmeyer: Senior Product Developer

Monica Kim: Senior Graphic Designer

FRUITMOJIS™

MIXED FRUIT-FLAVORED SNACKS
NATURALLY FLAVORED

60 POUCHES

U TALKIN' SNACK?!

SENSATIONS
BY COMPLIMENTS
COLD BREW

Retailer: Sobeys
Country: Canada
Category: G6. Beverages: Non-Alcoholic
Agency: Fish out of Water Design
Credits:
Brand Manager: Bonnie McCrone
Designer: Scott Pearson
Art Director: Sarah Grundy
Account Supervisor: Jennifer Harvey
Illustrator: Tim Murray

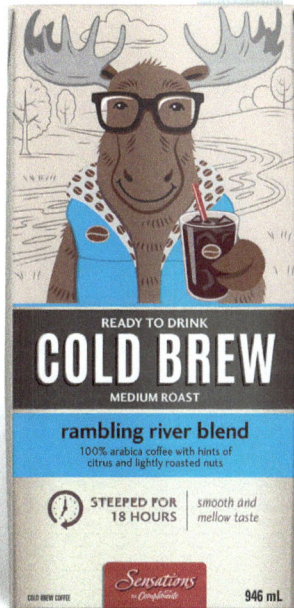

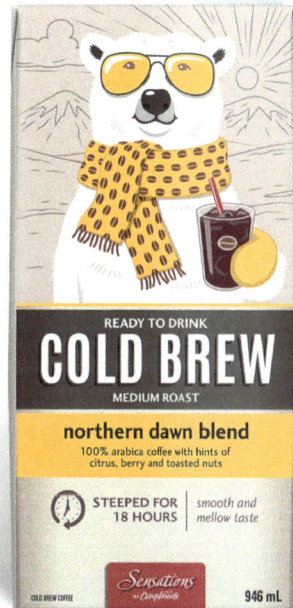

EL CORTE INGLÉS
BIO

Retailer: El Corte Inglés
Country: Spain
Category: B1. New Brand
Agency: Supperstudio
Credits:
Creative Director: Paco Adín
Account Director: Lourdes Morillas
Executive Manager: Susana Seijas.
Private Label Brand Manager El Corte Inglés: Jose Antonio Rojano

BiO
Zumo de Manzana
Sumo de Maça
Apple juice
SIN AZÚCARES AÑADIDOS
SIN SAL
SIN GRASA
Tortitas de Espelta
Bolachas de Espelta
Spelt Cakes
Selección de Frutos Secos
FUENTE DE FIBRA
Huevos frescos
Caldo de Pollo
Caldo de Frango
Chicken Broth
Smoothie naranja
Mermelada de fresa
Bebida de Avena
Bebida de Aveia
Oat drink
SIN LACTOSA
Fresa y Plátano
Banana y morango
Banana and strawberry
Bolitas de Arroz con Chocolate
FUENTE DE FIBRA

EL CORTE INGLÉS
TEX MEX

Retailer: El Corte Inglés

Country: Spain

Category: G3. Packaged Goods

Agency: Supperstudio

Credits:

Creative Director: Paco Adín

Account Director: Lourdes Morillas

Executive Manager: Susana Seijas.

Private Label Brand Manager El Corte Inglés: Jose Antonio Rojano

EL CORTE INGLÉS SNACKS

Retailer: El Corte Inglés
Country: Spain
Category: G3. Packaged Goods
Agency: Supperstudio
Credits:
Creative Director: Paco Adín
Account Director: Lourdes Morillas
Executive Manager: Susana Seijas.
Private Label Brand Manager El Corte Inglés: Jose Antonio Rojano

EL CORTE INGLÉS
BEERS

Retailer: El Corte Inglés
Country: Spain
Category: G5. Beverages: Alcoholic
Agency: Supperstudio
Credits:
Creative Director: Paco Adín
Account Director: Lourdes Morillas
Executive Manager: Susana Seijas.
Private Label Brand Manager El Corte Inglés: Jose Antonio Rojano

GUSTARE VITA

Retailer: Hy-Vee
Country: United States of America
Category: B1. New Brand
Agency: Meyocks
Credits:
The Hy-Vee – Meyocks Package Design Team

G'DAY

Retailer: Hy-Vee
Country: United States of America
Category: B1. New Brand
Agency: Meyocks
Credits:
The Hy-Vee – Meyocks Package Design Team

FRESH THYME
FRESH PIZZA

Retailer: Fresh Thyme
Country: United States of America
Category: G1. Fresh
Agency: The Creative Pack
Credits:
Creative Director: Danielle Beal
Designers & Illustrators: Heather Storie,
Corey Czer, Paola Ip, Emma Tung
Project Management: Fern Serna

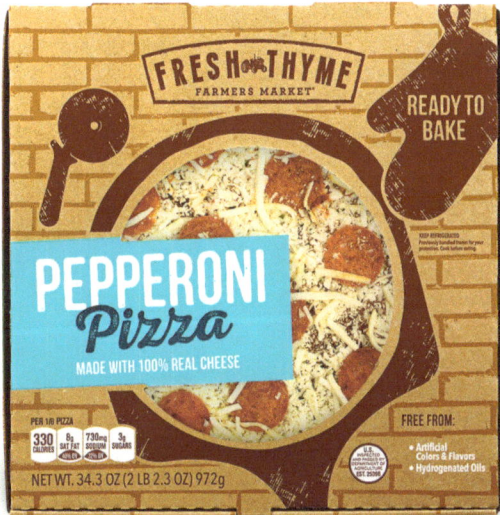

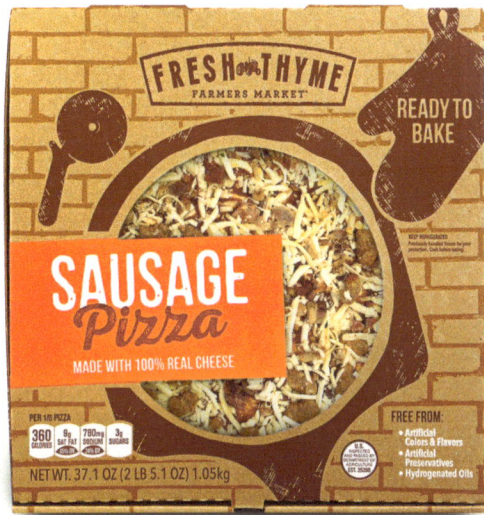

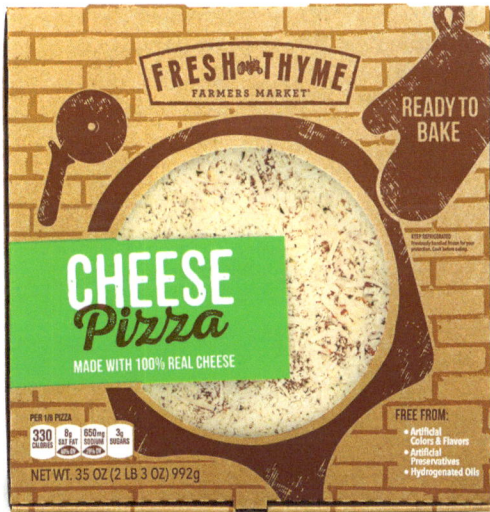

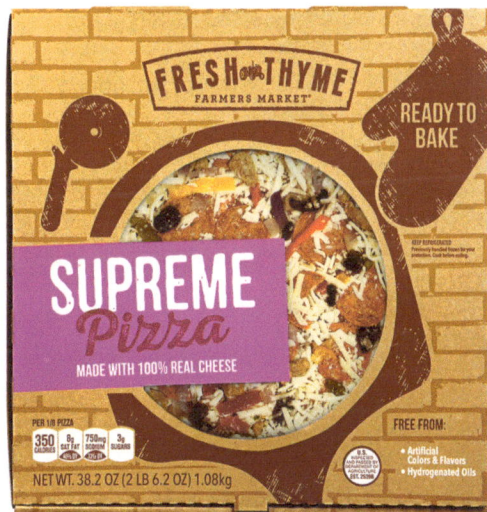

PRESTO!

Retailer: Amazon
Country: United States of America
Category: B1. New Brand
Agency: DDW
Credits:
Creative Director(s): Daniele Monti,
Ross Patrick
Designer: Eric Pino

BROOKSHIRE'S SEASONINGS

Retailer: Brookshire's
Country: United States of America
Category: G3. Packaged Goods
Agency: Daymon Creative Services
Credits:
Art Director: Elizabeth Santiago
Photographer: Autumn Underwood

LIVE
BETTER

Retailer: CVS Pharmacy, Inc.
Country: United States of America
Category: B1. New Brand
Agency: Wallace Church & Co.
Credits:
Creative Director Store Brand Portfolio, CVS Health: Gaemer Gutierrez
Executive Creative Director, Wallace Church: Stan Church
Creative Director, Wallace Church: John Bruno
Sr. Designer, Wallace: Diana Luistro
Strategist, Wallace Church: Michelle Sterns
Account Director, Wallace Church: Maureen McKenna

JUMBO
BATTERIES

Retailer: Jumbo Supermarkten N.V.
Country: The Netherlands
Category: H1. Home Cleaning
Agency: OD design studio
Credits:
Manager PL Jumbo: Frank van der Meij
Designer OD: Jeroen de Kok
Artwork: Jeroen de Kok

ALBERT HEIJN
SMOKED SAUSAGE

Retailer: Albert Heijn

Country: The Netherlands

Category: G3. Packaged Goods

Agency: Millford

Credits:

Account manager: Sascha Balk

Creative director: Jobert van de Bovenkamp

Art director: Jobert van de Bovenkamp

Designer: Jobert van de Bovenkamp

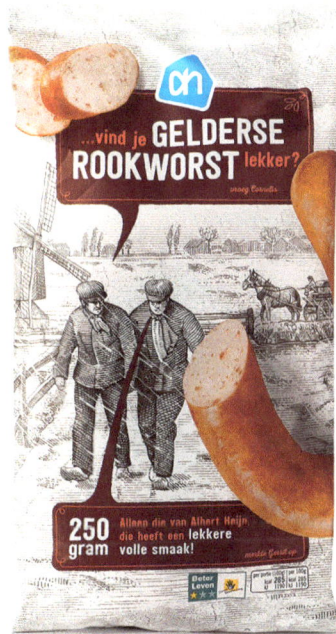
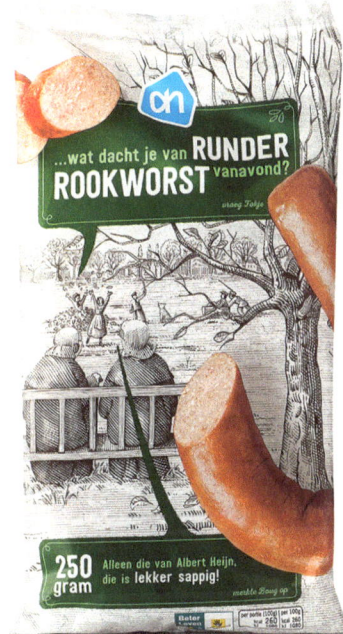

ALBERT HEIJN COOKING & DINING

Retailer: Albert Heijn
Country: The Netherlands
Category: H2. Home Care:
Agency: Millford
Credits:
Account manager: Sascha Balk
Creative director: Tahir Idouri
Art director: Tahir Idouri
Designer: Kim Kamperman

GARDE

KAASRASP

SPATEL

WATER GLAZEN
HOOGWAARDIG GLAS

IDEAAL OM
KOUDE DRANKEN
TE SERVEREN

2 STUKS | 40 CL

SNIJ PLANK
KUNST STOF
30 X 20 CM

KOEKEN PAN

XAVIER

Retailer: Action

Country: The Netherlands

Category: P3. Body Care

Agency: Yellow Dress Retail

Credits:

Brand manager client: Erwin Wentink,
Hans van Hattem, Ellen van Winkel

Designer: Tamas Paszto

Art director: Michelle Wiegman

MONOPRIX
FOOD TO GO

Retailer: Monoprix
Country: France
Category: B2. Redesigned Brand
Agency: Brandimage – Desgrippes & Laga
Credits:
Creative Director: Elie Hasbani
Art Director: Elodie Loisiel
Client Director: Marine Guillou

JUMBO WOOD OVEN PIZZAS

Retailer: Jumbo Supermarkten N.V.
Country: The Netherlands
Category: G1. Fresh
Agency: Od design studio
Credits:
Brand Manager Jumbo: Rik van der Loo
Concept: OD
Art Directors: Niels Alkema
Illustration & Typography: OD

JUMBO
ICE CREAM LOVERS

Retailer: Jumbo Supermarkten N.V.

Country: The Netherlands

Category: G4. Frozen

Agency: Od design studio

Credits:

Brand manager Jumbo: Frank van der Mei

Concept: OD

Art Directors: Jeroen de Kok

Typography: OD

JUMBO SPICES

Retailer: Jumbo Supermarkten N.V.

Country: The Netherlands

Category: G3. Packaged Goods

Agency: Od design studio

Credits:

Brand Manager Jumbo: Iris van den Berg

Concept: OD

Art Directors: Esther Baas

Photography: Peek Creative Studios

WOOLWORTHS CLEAN

Retailer: Woolworths
Country: Australia
Category: H1. Home Cleaning
Agency: Boxer & Co.
Credits:
Creative Director: Mark Haygarth
Project Manager - Boxer & Co.: Gwen Blake
Brand Owner – Sophie Challenor
Rollout – Marque

ALDI
RUNIK

Retailer: ALDI
Country: United States of America
Category: G5. Beverages: Alcoholic
Agency: Equator Design
Credits:
Designer: Mark Grey and Kasi Turpin
Creative Director: Jennifer Gaeto
Account Manager: Sarah Joyce
Account Director: Sophia Arconti

SILVER

UNIQUELY J FIG & THYME MINI CRISPS

Retailer: Jet.com
Country: United States of America
Category: G3. Packaged Goods
Agency: Elmwood
Credits:
Creative Director: Laura Kind

fig & thyme
mini crisps

PRINCE & SPRING
PRETZEL BITES

Retailer: Boxed

Country: United States of America

Category: G3. Packaged Goods

Agency: Prince & Spring

Credits:

Jeff Gamsey: VP of Private Brands

Chris Cheung: Creative Director

Vera Atamian: Designer

Annslee DeLuca: Brand Manager & Copy Writer

Brandon Wehmeyer: Senior Product Developer

Monica Kim: Senior Graphic Designer

PRINCE & SPRING™

PEANUT BUTTER
FILLED PRETZEL BITES

LOVE AT FIRST BITE

NET WT 44 OZ (2 LB 12 OZ) 1.24kg

GREAT VALUE ICE CREAM CONES

Retailer: Walmart
Country: United States of America
Category: G3. Packaged Goods
Agency: Parker Williams
Credits:
Creative Director: Jo Saker
Design Director: Andrew Cole
Account Director: Samantha Lee
Senior Account Manager: Christoforou Christoforou
Walmart Design Lead: Sarah Paskell

ALIADA

Retailer: El Corte Inglés
Country: Spain
Category: B1. New Brand
Agency: Supperstudio
Credits
Creative Director: Paco Adín
Account Director: Lourdes Morillas
Executive Manager: Susana Seijas.

Néctar de Naranja

• A BASE DE CONCENTRADO
• CONTENIDO DE FRUTA MÍNIMO 50%
• CON EDULCORANTES

Néctar de laranja proveniente de concentrado. Teor mínimo de frutas: 50%. Com edulcorantes

1 Litro

Leche entera

Leite gordo
Whole milk

1 Litro

Pañales recién nacido

Newborn diapers
Fraldas recém-nascidos

3-6 kilos   40 unidades

Palitos de Surimi
SABOR MARISCO

EL CORTE INGLÉS GAZPACHO

Retailer: El Corte Inglés
Country: Spain
Category: B1. New Brand
Agency: Supperstudio
Credits:
Creative Director: Paco Adín
Account Director: Lourdes Morillas
Executive Manager: Susana Seijas.

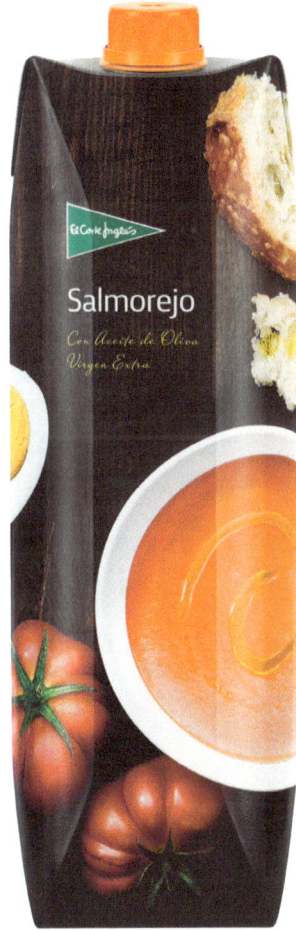

EL CORTE INGLÉS
PANETTONE

Retailer: El Corte Inglés

Country: Spain

Category: B4. Holiday or Limited Edition

Agency: tridimage

Credits:

Brand Manager: José Antonio Rojano López

Design Directors: Adriana Cortese, Hernán Braberman, Virginia Gines

Project Manager: Guillermo Dufranc

Art Director: Natalia Gioiosa

CULINARY TOURS

Brand: Culinary Tours
Retailer: Participating Topco Member Retailers
Country: United States of America
Category: B1. New Brand
Agency: Topco Associates
Credits:
Creative Director: Shelbi Sturges
Lead Designer: Kara Fleming-Ward
Designers: Kathy Kolba, Brian Carron,
Hedy Wong, Mindy Syster

LIMITED TIME ORIGINALS HOLIDAY

Retailer: Giant / Stop & Shop
Country: United States of America
Category: B4. Holiday or Limited Edition Private Brand
Agency: Ahold Own Brands Design
Credits:
Senior Vice President, Own Brands: Juan De Paoli
Creative Director, Designer: Paul Skozilas
Director of Merchandising: Mark Gilliand
Director of Brand Management: Kasey Sheffer

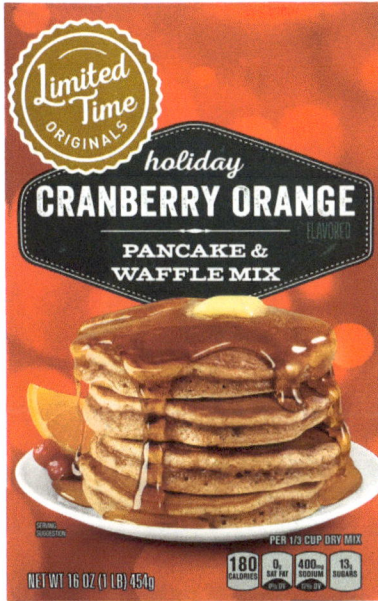

BACK TO COLLEGE 2017

Retailer: Bed Bath & Beyond
Country: United States of America
Category: B4. Holiday or Limited Edition
Agency: Invok Brands
Credits:
VP Packaging and Graphics, Bed Bath & Beyond: Roopi Crowley
Partner/Chief Creative Officer, Invok Brands: Richard Shear
Designer, Invok Brands: Nikki Nardi

EQUIP YOUR SPACE

CLIP LAMP

MATTE WHITE

FEATURES TO THE MAX
ADJUSTABLE GOOSENECK
CLIP TO YOUR HEADBOARD
OR DESK

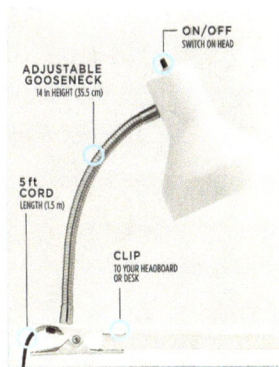

ON/OFF
SWITCH ON HEAD

ADJUSTABLE
GOOSENECK
14 in HEIGHT (35.5 cm)

5 ft
CORD
LENGTH (1.5 m)

CLIP
TO YOUR HEADBOARD
OR DESK

EQUIP YOUR SPACE

CLIP LAMP   MATTE WHITE

ENERGY SAVINGS

BRIGHTNESS

MARKET DISTRICT
COFFEE

Retailer: Giant Eagle
Country: United States of America
Category: G3. Packaged Goods
Agency: Daymon Creative Services
Credits:
Designer: Tiffany London
Photographer: Autumn Underwood

MARKET DISTRICT
MEDIUM ROAST
BREAKFAST
100% ARABICA
COFFEE BLEND
Bright, balanced blend
with a crisp finish
ground
coffee
NET WT
12 OZ (340g)
RAINFOREST ALLIANCE CERTIFIED
30% Certified Coffee

FRESH DIRECT
JUST NUT BARS

Retailer: Fresh Direct
Country: United States of America
Category: G3. Packaged Goods
Agency: Daymon Creative Services
Credits:
Art Director: Kaitlin Herrmann
Photographer: Autumn Underwood

SIMPLY ME
BEAUTY

Retailer: 7-Eleven
Country: United States of America
Category: P4. Beauty: perfumes, cosmetics, make-up, etc.
Agency: Brandimage
Credits:
Executive Creative Director: Don Childs
Art Director: Scott Smith
Designer: Jeff Raulie & Amanda Denhart
Production Artist: Ree Foltz
Brand Managers: Jenny Price & Anna Oris

7-SELECT
GO!SMART COLD
PRESSED JUICE

Retailer: 7-Eleven
Country: United States of America
Category: G6. Beverages: Non-Alcoholic
Agency: Brandimage
Credits:
Executive Creative Director: Don Childs
Art Director: Scott Smith
Designer: Scott Smith
Production Artist: Ree Foltz
Brand Managers: Jenny Price & Anna Oris

NATURAL
GOODNESS

Retailer: The Dairy Farm Group
Country: Asia Pacific
Category: B1. New Brand
Agency: Muse Creative
Credits:
Own Brand Director: Fann Yuen
Brand Manager: Chris Leung
Creative Director: Iris Lee
Graphic Designer: Jeslyn Tai & Amelie Yap

AQUABLISS
PERSONAL CARE

Retailer: The Dairy Farm Group
Country: Asia Pacific
Category: B1. New Brand
Agency: Brand Chef
Credits:
Own Brand Director: Fann Yuen
Head of Brand Marketing: Susanne Migchels
Brand Manager: Stephanie Lau
Design Project Manager: Tse Chun Kit
Principal & Creative Director: Sugil Lee

PRINCE & SPRING
COCONUT WATER

Retailer: Boxed

Country: United States

Category: G6. Beverages: Non-Alcoholic

Agency: Boxed

Credits:

VP Private Brands: Jeff Gamsey

Creative Director: Chris Cheung

Senior Packaging Designer: Vera Atamian

Brand Manager / Copywriter: Annslee DeLuca

JUMBO
FRESH JUICES

Retailer: Jumbo Supermarkten N.V.
Country: The Netherlands
Category: G1. Fresh
Agency: OD design studio
Credits:
Brand Manager Jumbo: Sabine Snijders-Simons
Concept: OD
Art Directors: Lotje Nieuwenhuis, Niels Alkem
Typography: OD

LEAPS & BOUNDS
TOYS

Retailer: Petco and Unleashed by Petco
Country: United States of America
Category: B2. Redesigned Brand
Agency: Periscope & Petco Animal Supplies, Inc.
Credits:
Art Director: Francesca Mahoney
Brand Director: Francesca Mahoney
Creative Directors: Richard Gordon-Smith, Rob Peichel
Designer: Shayla Nesheim
Illustration: Richard Gordon-Smith
Copywriting: Peter Ripple
Packaging Engineer: Peter Foltz
Production Artist: Nicholas Possedi
Photographer (product): OneKreate
Photographer (packaging): Petco In-House Photography studio
Printer: Ningbo Fenghua Sinso Printing Co., Ltd.

PADERNO

Retailer: Canadian Tire
Country: Canada
Category: B2. Redesigned Brand
Agency: Concrete
Credits:
Brand Manager: Unha Park
Associate Brand Manager: Emma Horner
Packaging Manager: Angela Stone
Packaging Consultant: Candice Noble
Structural Packaging: Oksana Lapierre
Creative direction (agency): Diti Katona, John Pylypczak

IRRESISTIBLES SMOOTHIE MIX

Retailer: Metro s.e.n.c.

Country: Canada

Category: G4, Frozen

Agency: Pigeon brands

Credits:

Client: Metro s.e.n.c

Director, design, and packaging: Marie Horodecki-Aymes

Design and branding creative direction manager: Eric Gagnon

Agency: Pigeon

Creative director: Olivier Chevillot

Designer: Jessika Neal

Group account director: Armelle Dubourg

Production director: Phillippe Morin

Photographer: Christian Lacroix

Prepress: SGS

Printer: Flexipak

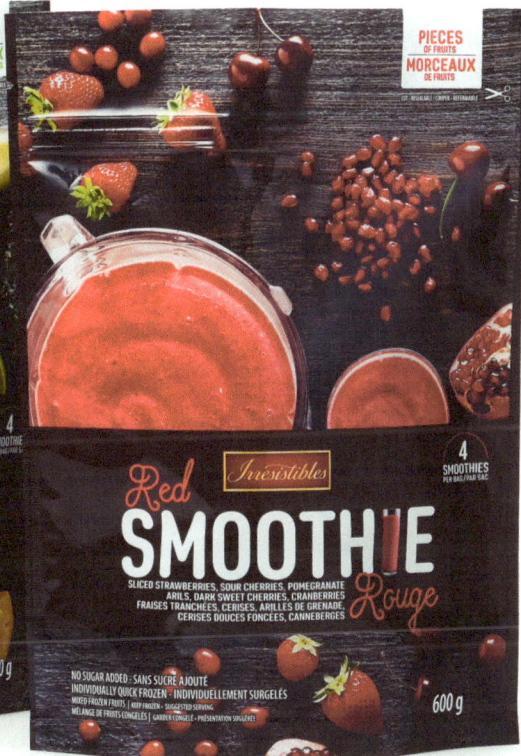

IRRESISTIBLES GLOW IN THE DARK TISSUE

Retailer: Metro s.e.n.c.

Country: Canada

Category: P2. Health Care

Agency: Pigeon brands

Credits:

Client: Metro s.e.n.c.

Director, design and packaging: Marie Horodecki-Aymes

Design and branding creative direction manager: Eric Gagnon

Agency: Pigeon

Creative director: Olivier Chevillot

Designer: Jessika Neal

Group account director: Armelle Dubourg

Production director: Phillippe Morin

Prepress: SGS Co (Montréal)

Printer: WestRock (Warwick)

WOOLWORTHS GOLD

Retailer: Woolworths
Country: Australia
Category: B2. Redesigned Brand
Agency: Boxer & Co.
Credits:
Creative Director: Mark Haygarth
Brand Manager: Olivia Hadlow
Project Manager (agency): Gwen Blake
Photography and roll-out: Marque

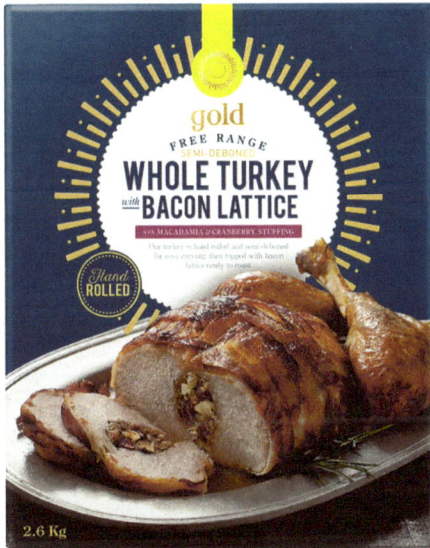

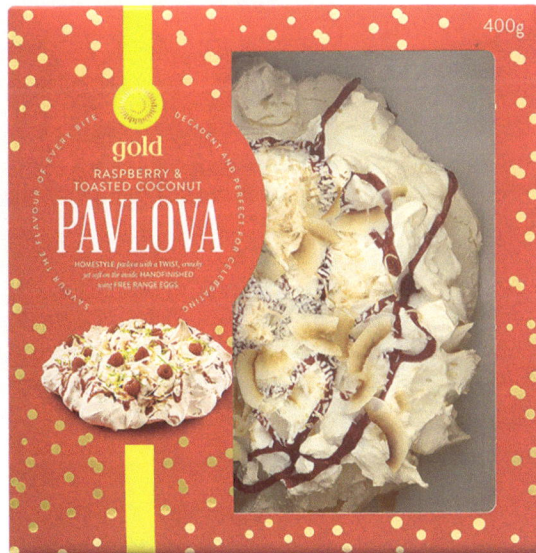

MEMBER'S MARK
ORGANIC MILK

Retailer: Sam's Club
Country: United States of America
Category: G1. Fresh
Agency: Equator Design
Credits:
Designer: Erica Johnstone
Creative Director: Michael Duffy
Account Manager: Malia Jollenbeck

CONSUM
JAM

Retailer: Supermercados Consum

Country: Spain

Category: G3. Packaged Goods

Agency: Agencia Maslow SL

Credits:

Account Directors: Managing Directors: Marta Álvarez / Ana Niño

Strategic Planning: Ana Niño

Creative Director: Pau Rodilla

Art Director: Africa Leiva

BRONZE

MACRO

Retailer: Woolworths

Country: Australia

Category: B2. Redesigned Brand

Agency: Marque Brand Consultants

Credits:

Brand Strategy: Marcel Wijnen, Lynette Sandhu

Design team: Marcel Wijnen. Stacey Ayers,
Polly Barton, Jess Parisi

Writer: Lynette Sandhu

Design Realisation: Steve Hoffman, Peita Neale,
Ed Graves, Don Reynolds

Project Manager: Suzi Della-Pietra, Blanca Veiga

Woolworths Brand Team: Rachel Pryce,
Kate Walker, Jade Tonkin

UNIQUELY J
AVOCADO OIL

Retailer: Jet.com
Country: United States of America
Category: G3. Packaged Goods
Agency: Elmwood
Credits:
Creative Director, Laura Kind

UNIQUELY J
CLEANER

Retailer: Jet.com
Country: United States of America
Category: H1. Home Cleaning
Agency: Elmwood
Credits:
Creative Director, Laura Kind

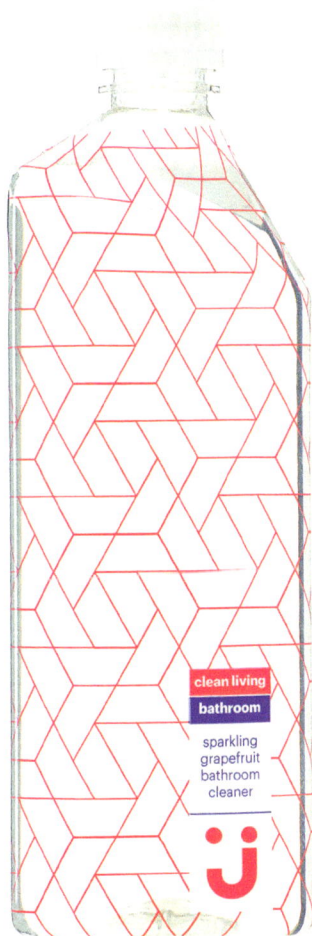

clean living

bathroom

sparkling
grapefruit
bathroom
cleaner

SAM'S CHOICE ITALIA

Retailer: Walmart
Country: United States of America
Category: B1. New Brand
Agency: Anthem
Credits:
Creative Director: Gerard Rizzo
Design Director: Tracey Ujfalussy
Account Director: Bernadette Sheppard, Leigh Waycaster
Photographer: Wak Pictures, Susan Kinast
Walmart Design Lead: Sarah Paskell

SAM'S CHOICE COFFEE

Retailer: Walmart
Country: United States of America
Category: G3. Packaged Goods
Agency: Anthem
Credits:
Creative Director: Helena Yoon
Design Director: Tracey Ujfalussy
Account Director: Bernadette Sheppard, Leigh Waycaster
Walmart Design Lead: Sarah Paskell

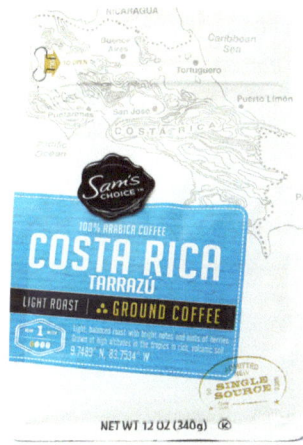

PRINCE & SPRING
EPSOM SALTS

Retailer: Boxed
Country: United States
Category: B1. New Brand
Agency: Prince & Spring
Credits:
VP of Private Brands: Jeff Gamsey
Creative Director: Chris Cheung
Senior Designer: Vera Atamian
Brand Manager & Copy Writer: Annslee DeLuca
Senior Product Developer: Brandon Wehmeyer
Graphic Designer: Monica Kim
Illustrator: David Kim

PRINCE & SPRING™

LAVENDER-SCENTED

EPSOM SALT

SOAKING AID

LAVENDAAAAAHHH
NET WT. 3 LB (1.36kg)

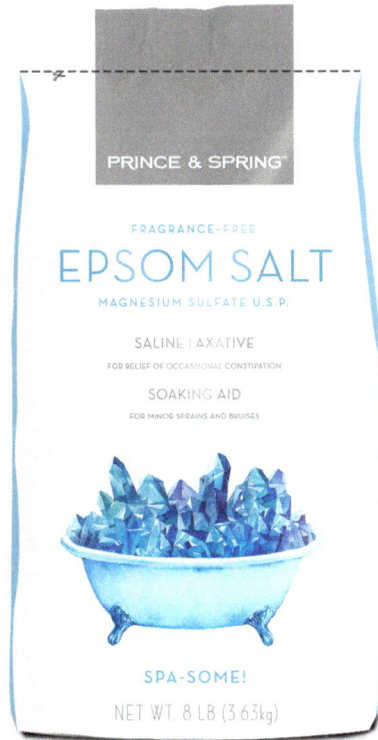

PRINCE & SPRING™

FRAGRANCE-FREE

EPSOM SALT

MAGNESIUM SULFATE U.S.P.

SALINE LAXATIVE
FOR RELIEF OF OCCASIONAL CONSTIPATION

SOAKING AID
FOR MINOR SPRAINS AND BRUISES

SPA-SOME!
NET WT. 8 LB (3.63kg)

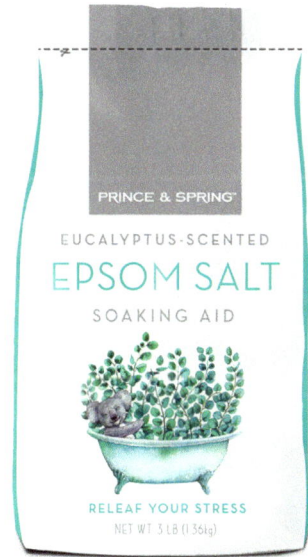

PRINCE & SPRING™

EUCALYPTUS-SCENTED

EPSOM SALT

SOAKING AID

RELEAF YOUR STRESS
NET WT. 3 LB (1.36kg)

EARTH FARE
SELTZER WATER

Retailer: Earth Fare
Country: United States
Category: G6. Beverages: Non-Alcoholic
Agency: SailPointe Creative Group
Credits:
Director of Private Brands Earth Fare: Chris Slick
Private Brand and Product Development Marketer Earth Fare: Scott Lindsay
Private Brands Category Manager Earth Fare: Katlin Pickering
Purchasing Support Coordinator Earth Fare: Elizabeth Stephens
VP of Brand Management SailPointe Creative: Jen Linke
Art Director SailPointe Creative: Kevin Keene
Sr. Designer & Illustrator SailPointe Creative: Robert Rios
Production Artist: Angie Wdowiak
Account Manager SailPointe Creative: Lynne Traci

GIANT/STOP & SHOP PASTA SAUCE

Retailer: Giant / Stop & Shop
Country: United States
Category: G3. Packaged Goods
Agency: Ahold Own Brands Design
Credits:
Senior Vice President, Own Brands: Juan De Paoli
Creative Director, Designer: Paul Skozilas
Director of Merchandising: Mark Gilliand
Director of Brand Management: Kasey Sheffer

ETOS
FACE MASK

Retailer: Giant / Stop & Shop
Country: United States of America
Category: P4. Beauty: perfumes, cosmetics, make-up, etc.
Agency: Ahold Own Brands Design
Credits:
Senior Vice President, Own Brands: Juan De Paoli
Creative Director, Designer: Paul Skozilas
Director of Merchandising: Mark Gilliand
Director of Brand Management: Kasey Sheffer

PERSONNELLE
DEPILATORY

Retailer: Jean Coutu Group
Country: Canada
Category: P3. Body Care
Agency: Cabana Séguin inc.
Credits:
Brand Manager: Guy Jinchereau
Creative Direction: Martine Gadbois
Art Director: Valérie Fouché
Graphic Designer: Eve Paquet
Illustrator: Stéphane Geoffrion
Account Director: Andrea Lange
Production Manager: Marc Dufresne

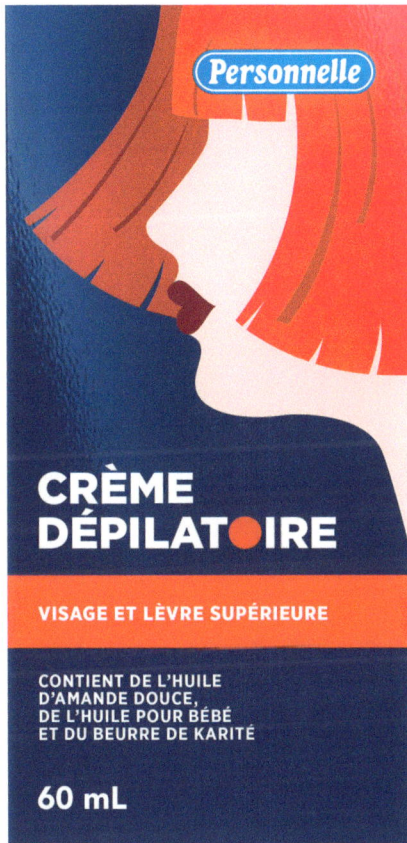

CLUB DEL GOURMET
CURED FISH

Retailer: El Corte Inglés
Country: Spain
Category: G1. Fresh
Agency: tridimage
Credits:
Brand Manager: José Antonio Rojano López
Design Directors: Adriana Cortese, Hernán Braberman, Virginia Gines
Project Manager: Guillermo Dufranc
Art Director: Pablo Iotti
Illustrator: Maya Pixelskaya

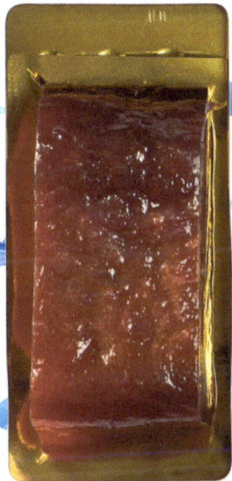

Mojama de Atún
Extra en taco
Mojama de atún extra en bloc. Extra cured tuna loin block.

Hueva de Mújol
en Taco
Ova de tainha. Grey mullet roe.

Huevas de Atunarro
en Taco
Ovas de atum solareiro. Yellowfin tuna roe.

FRESH THYME
TASTY TYKES

Retailer: Fresh Thyme
Country: United States of America
Category: B1. New Brand
Agency: The Creative Pack
Credits:
Creative Director: Danielle Beal
Designers & Illustrators: Heather Storie, Corey Czer, Paola Ip, Emma Tung
Project Management: Fern Serna

FRESH THYME
FREEZE DRIED FRUIT

Retailer: Fresh Thyme
Country: United States of America
Category: G3. Packaged Goods
Agency: The Creative Pack
Credits:
Creative Director: Danielle Beal
Designers & Illustrators: Heather Storie, Corey Czer, Paola Ip, Emma Tung
Project Management: Fern Serna

NICE!

Retailer: Walgreens
Country: United States of America
Category: B2. Redesigned Brand
Agency: Soulsight/Walgreens
Credits:
Walgreens Boots Alliance
Senior Brand Manager: Jodi Kier
Senior Director Brand Management/Product Development: Nancy Garver
Senior Manager, Owned Brands Research: Laura Zoller
Group Vice President: Helayna Minsk
Soulsight
Partner, Chief Strategy Officer: James Pietruszynski
Associate Account Strategy Manager: Delanie Carney
Creative Director: Stephanie Crair
Senior Account + Strategy Manager: Jessica Feld

HT TRADERS
GRANOLA

Retailer: Harris Teeter
Country: United States
Category: G3. Packaged Goods
Agency: Harris Teeter Daymon Creative Services
Credits:
Senior Design Manager: Felix Rosales
Photographer: Autumn Underwood
Director of Advertising & Creative: Steve Kent
Marketing Manager: Kim Davis
Director of Private Brands: Charles Brame

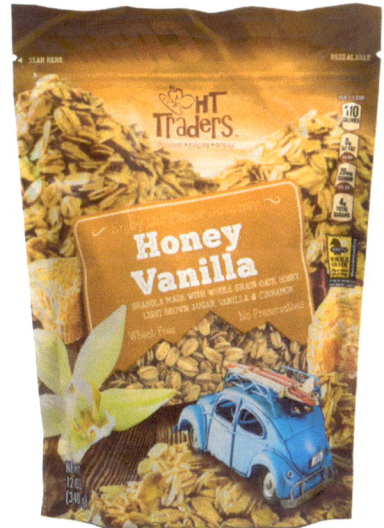

7-SELECT GO!YUM COLD BREW COFFEE

Retailer: 7-Eleven

Country: United States

Category: G6. Beverages: Non-Alcoholic

Agency: Brandimage

Credits:

Executive Creative Director: Don Childs

Art Director: Scott Smith

Designer: Jeff Raulie

Production Artist: Ree Foltz

Brand Managers: Jenny Price & Anna Oris

NATURAL GROCERS

Retailer: Natural Grocers
Country: United States
Category: B1. New Brand
Agency: MBD
Credits:
Art Director: Sandra Button
Designer: Becca Marco
Creative Director: Steve Martin
Production Artist: Angie Beighle, Dan Cosco
Account Director: Jennifer Banton
Project Manager: Ivana Baric
Brand Manager: Kevin Miller

WELLSLEY FARMS SPICES

Retailer: BJ's Wholesale Club
Country: United States of America
Category: G3. Packaged Goods
Agency: MBD
Credits:
Art Director: Tracy Lemere
Production Artist: Deanna Vosburgh
Account Director: Maria Dubuc
Project Manager: Alison Hom

PNP
TINY TOTS

Retailer: Pick n Pay
Country: South Africa
Category: P5. Baby
Agency: Daymon
Credits:
Creative Direction: Jens Sievert
Design: Inês de Almeida Batista
Account Executive: Inês Santos

LIVE
WELL

Retailer: Pick n Pay
Country: South Africa
Category: B1. New Brand
Agency: Daymon
Credits:
Design: Sigbjorn Gjennestad
Account Executive: Ines Santos, Nadieha Petersen

LIVE WELL

JELLY
ORANGE
FLAVOURED

PnP

LIVE WELL

WHOLE WHEAT
LASAGNE SHEETS

High in Fibre

REDUCED
SUGAR

SERVING
SUGGESTION 250 g

LIVE WELL

PnP

BUTTERNUT
SOUP

with a hint
of coriander

LOW
FAT

REDUCED
SALT

LIVE WELL

PnP

STRAW-
BERRY
JAM

REDUCED
SUGAR

450 g

LIVE WELL

PnP

LITE
GREEK
VINAIGRETTE

LOW
FAT

340 ml

PICK
LOCAL

Retailer: Pick n Pay
Country: South Africa
Category: B1. New Brand
Agency: Daymon
Credits:
Creative Direction: Jens Sievert
Design: Carina Sousa, Katlego Matabane
Account Executive: Margarida Lacerda, Nadieha Petersen
Final Artist: Josiah Tsokedi, Devon Ford

LOCALLY PRODUCED
Pick Local
SUPPORTING SMALL BUSINESS

PnP

Zoegdie and Bilqees Essa started out their company manufacturing flavoured popcorn and then branched into manufacturing "Flatbreads of the world". Comassa Food Services was born and they fulfilled their dream to grow their business and also to give back to the community that they work in.

White Tortilla Wrap

Locally Sourced & Packed

6's

Energy 588 kJ

7%

LOCALLY PRODUCED
Pick Local
SUPPORTING SMALL BUSINESS

PnP

Black Olives

Goedgedacht Trading, nestled in the Western Cape & Riebeeksriver Valley, is the producer of quality extra virgin olive oil and fruit-infused dressings and is fully owned by The Goedgedacht Trust, a rural non-profit organisation, established on the farm in 1993.

Scan code for our story

Locally Sourced & Packed
200 g net
100 g drained
CHOICE GRADE

Per serving:
Energy 145 kJ
2%
of adult GDA*

Pesto
Black Olive & Tomato

Sage Kitchen, the brainchild of husband and wife duo Beverly and ... started as a small business in their home kitchen when they saw an opportunity to live their passion through creating small jars of flavour innovations. They employ staff from the local community to help them make their dreams a reality and create delectable pesto products.

PnP

Energy 188 kJ
2%
of adult GDA*

130 g

PnP

Edward Moshole, founder of Chem-Fresh products was working as a cleaner when he identified a need for gentle detergents made from quality ingredients. From this he started his company and handled all the manufacturing himself, using a handmade mixer set up in his backyard, while selling his detergents —door to door.

Scan code for our story

ml

PINGO DOCE
PASTA

Retailer: Pingo Doce
Country: Portugal
Category: G3. Packaged Goods
Agency: Daymon
Credits:
Creative Direction: Jens Sievert
Design: Catarina Almeida
Account Executive: Lucia Coelho

PAMS
FINEST

Retailer: Foodstuffs Own Brands Ltd.
Country: New Zealand
Category: B1. New Brand
Agency: Brother Design
Credits:
Art Director & Designer: Paula Bunny
Designers: Mahani Jones, Justine Rankine, Kirsty Harvey
Account Managers: Nicole Blackwood, Jenny McMillan
Photographers: Shaun Cato-Symonds, Melanie Jenkins
Stylist: Jo Wilcox, Jo Bridgford, Julie Le Clerc

FAIRWAY MARKET
GRASS-FED MILKS

Retailer: Fairway Market
Country: USA
Category: G2: Organic and Natural food
Agency: Nancy Frame Design
Credits:
Nancy Frame: Creative Director
Emanuel Guillermo: Designer
Bob Frame: Copy Writer

5 QUESTIONS

DAVID ZIEGLER-VOLL

Creative Director, MBD
Boston, Massachussets

Over the last year Amazon, Whole Foods, Lidl, and Jet have made aggressive moves into private brand, what impact are you seeing them have on your private brand clients and their brands?

There is no doubt that new-comers to private brand are pushing the design envelope. There is less attachment to "brand-ego" and more emphasis on creating experiences that transcend a brand book. The reality is retailers, such as Jet, speak the language of younger audiences and they execute this through fresh, invigorating design. Retailers are suddenly competing in a landscape of what is or isn't Instagrammed; what makes or doesn't make the front page of PopSugar. This breath of fresh air is a very good thing for private brands as it's forcing retailers to evaluate how they're telling their story.

What role should strategy play in solving retail problems?

I'm a big believer in sketching before attempting a design. Additionally, I ask a minimum of 5,932 questions because I want to fully and completely understand the design problem that I am solving. Strategy is really no different. Retailers should expect their private brand team to be inquisitive, curious and not afraid to ask tough questions. In turn, creative teams should be expected to synthesize these answers into real and meaningful solutions.

What are the most common mistake retailers make with their brands?

It's imperative that retailers understand that a one-size-fits-all approach to brand integration is confusing, and quite frankly, dreadfully boring. Trying to force the same brand attributes of a bag of potato chips onto a bottle of scotch does nothing for the product or the brand.

What advice do you have for retailers trying to take their brands to the next level?

Retailers should think of their private brand guidelines as just that, guidelines and not the letter of the law. Successful private brand products should be able to tell a story specific to its audience while simultaneously living within its brand eco-system. While brand guidelines certainly have their purpose, creating stunning and compelling stories can only exlst If retailers relax their "brand-ego". I would also encourage retailers to embrace one of the most amazing attributes of private brand... it's an incredibly nimble business that can easily be tweaked as attitudes and audiences change over time.

What will private brands look like 10 years from now?

Much like Trader Joe's, I think we are going to see less emphasis on what constitutes private brand or private label. From a design perspective, I think we are going to see less heavily branded package design, e.g. Trader Joe's for the most part only utilizes a single logo as a "brand" element and they are incontrovertibly one of the most successful "private" label grocers in the country.

ZHOU WENJUN

Founder, Creative Director & Architect of 524 Studio
China

Over the last year Amazon, Whole Foods, Lidl, and Jet have made aggressive moves into private brand, what impact are you seeing them have on your private brand clients and their brands?

Private brand is compared with traditional manufacturer brand. With relatively low costs and relatively high returns, developing own brand has become a trend that cannot be ignored and an important part of composition of profits for retailers. Actually, both in China and abroad, whether it's a traditional well-known brand or a new private brand, businessmen invest a big cost in the aspect such as the environment decorates, but there is a great lack of investment in brand packaging, visual design, etc. For our private brand clients, they produce self-produced goods, eliminate many intermediate links, save a lot of advertising expenses. They can carry out mass production and sales, achieve economies of scale and reduce the cost of selling goods.

What role should strategy play in solving retail problems?

The strategy is the direction. A good strategy is conducive to enhance the competitiveness of commodities. It's beneficial to form characteristic management, give full play to the advantages of intangible assets, have more autonomy, accurately grasp the market demand, improve the management level of retail enterprises..

What are the most common mistake retailers make with their brands?

To reduce market risk, some retailers have launched a number of own-brand products that mimic manufacturers' brands to mislead consumers. Their brands lack independent design strategies and lack strategic investment in design. These actions may infringe on the intellectual property of others. In other words, product brands and quality are difficult to guarantee. I remember that Mr. Jack Ma, founder of the Alibaba Group, who said that everyone should have zero tolerance for violations of the intellectual property.

What advice do you have for retailers trying to take their brands to the next level?

For private brand, it is impossible to succeed if positioning is not clear. It's not necessarily only on the basis of price, but also on product quality, packaging design and brand design, they are also important too. The essence of the brand is the product, the product meets the needs of the consumer, and the brand satisfies the consumer's desire. So, I think that private brands need to increase strategic investment in design strategies. Once the market positioning of the private brand is clear, the business characteristics of the enterprise will be formed accordingly.

What will private brands look like 10 years from now?

In the next decade, online, offline and logistics could be combined more organic. Private brands will have a huge impact on brands that are based on traditional and mature retail business models. And more excellent design would help more and more private brands to better themselves. The successful private brands can grasp more initiative of competition. Well, let's see it!

MARIA DUBUC

Maria Dubuc, President, MBD
Boston, Massachussets

Over the last year Amazon, Whole Foods, Lidl, and Jet have made aggressive moves into private brand, what impact are you seeing them have on your private brand clients and their brands?

They're changing the whole landscape. We're seeing some major shifts from our clients. Retailers are no longer sticking their heads in the sand when it comes to their brands; instead they're looking at ways to improve. They're upping their games in order to compete with the new and expanding players. It's really exciting because as creatives, there's so much we're going to be able to do with building brands now – better, innovative design, more emphasis on strategy, watching trends and making them, not just reacting to them. Our clients are seeing the impact of investing in their brands. It's exciting, and it's about time!

What role should strategy play in solving retail problems?

If you don't have a plan, you're not going anywhere or you have no idea were you are going. That's a problem, so having a strategy is key. There was a time when the only plan for most retailers was to carry low-cost national brand equivalents. There was no marketing, no strategy. Just have them. In many cases, the brand was created by a contract graphic artist doing what he liked, with no consideration for the consumer. Those days are over, and private brand is never going back to that. The reality today is that retailers must have a brand-specific strategy in order to be noticed in today's marketplace. It needs to be created by someone who understands your consumer, product mix, and company, so your brands end up being your customer's first choice, not a choice.

What are the most common mistake retailers make with their brands?

Retailers need to stop talking to themselves. It's not about what you like. It's about what consumers like. And if you're using a creative look from 30 years ago, they're not going to like you. Conversely, you can't create a strategy that focuses on one universal look across all channels to be used for the next 10 years. There's constant evolution in the industry, especially today, when competition is becoming fierce. Private brand strategy has to be creative, and it has to be consumer-centric. Always remember, they're the ones you're trying to reach.

What advice do you have for retailers trying to take their brands to the next level?

Be flexible and nimble! Have a strategy, but keep an eye on the trends. Your strategy should be adaptable and have evolution built into its DNA. Consumers don't stay the same for five years. Retailers can't either. Agencies know the rules of design, communication, and branding. Trust yours to know when it's okay to break the rules because it's their job to be agile and have their ear to the ground. If you don't trust them, it's time for a new agency.

What will private brands look like 10 years from now?

I'm convinced the industry is only going to get better. If you went to the Velocity conference, or you've read Vanguard Vintage Originals, you know there was a time when private brand was amazing. There weren't national brands and private brands. There were just brands. I'm happy to say, we're going back to simply building great brands. Ten years from now, we'll all be taking chances with our brands and designs, because why not take risks and chances? We own the brands. Ten years from now, the concept of "private" brands will be archaic, because we're going to change that attitude. It's time to drop the word "private" and be what we are: brands!

DON CHILDS

SVP, Executive Creative Director, BrandImage
Ohio, USA

Over the last year Amazon, Whole Foods, Lidl, and Jet have made aggressive moves into private brand, what impact are you seeing them have on your private brand clients and their brands?

I see a few ways our private brand clients are looking for ways to compete with the national brands and new online retailers. They're evaluating and refining their strategies and striving to innovate on their strategic vectors rather than emulate others'. They're also spending more time seeking shopper and customer insights and putting innovations in place that fulfill their unmet needs. Lastly, I see them investing in design as a strategic way to gain the competitive advantage like never before

What role should strategy play in solving retail problems?

The historical challenge of private brands is that they tend to react and respond, often following a national brand's lead. Strategy is the tool that allows private brands to take control of their own destiny and set a path toward the future that supports their overarching strategic goals. Strategy is the roadmap that allows a retailer to set their own course rather than run about following others. Strategy is key to building strong private brands that can compete with and at times dominate national brands. It should support organizational agility allowing timely decisions versus hasty ones. In short, it feels like a cultural shift toward a proactive climate of "what's next!" rather than "what do we do now?".

What are the most common mistake retailers make with their brands?

Setting a strategy and sticking to it seems very difficult for a lot of retailers – they suffer from reactionary brand proliferation. There's a tendency to try to be everything to everyone, to chase trends, to mimic the market instead of focusing on building their own meaningful and motivating brand solutions. While the strength of the retailer is its ability to act quickly, in the effort to be relevant or communicate value, they are often being short-sighted, ending up with diluted and meaningless brands. Figure out who you are and why you exist – act more like marketers than merchandisers.

What advice do you have for retailers trying to take their brands to the next level?

Design is the voice of your private brand and usually the only touchpoint in the marketing mix your customer is guaranteed to engage with. So it stands to reason that Design is not a cost to manage, it's a strategic tool to invest in. Invest time in doing it right, invest in customer insights, brand architecture, brand strategy, developing a meaningful story and invest in the expression of your brand. Some CPGs are going the wrong way, away from the power of design and the value it plays in brand choice and loyalty.

What will private brands look like 10 years from now?

CPGs have not done a good job responding to the threat of private brands. Many are plodding behemoths who treat their "equities" as anchors rather than springboards. I've seen little indication this will change. They're cutting-cost to try to find their way to growth and profitability. The trend that finds CPGs reacting to innovations coming from retailers is a signal of what's ahead for private brands. Private brands will be the ones who define what it means to be a brand. Retailers will be the benchmark for consumer experience, agility and innovation.

NICK VAUS

Partner & Creative Director, DewGibbons + Partners
United Kingdom

Over the last year Amazon, Whole Foods, Lidl, and Jet have made aggressive moves into private brand, what impact are you seeing them have on your private brand clients and their brands?

Let's face it, when Amazon makes any kind of aggressive move, it affects everyone. My agency works with both private brand retailers in the UK/Europe and global branded clients, and the impact of increasing penetration into private brand by the likes of Amazon, Whole Foods, and Lidl has made all our clients sharper, more focused, and on their toes.

There's definitely a move towards better understanding consumers and delivering innovation, whether that's through new products or through the marketing and design of the products. But the truth is that the innovation side of things is less apparent with private brands. Retailers operate on such narrow margins, so can they really afford to invest in private brand innovation to truly become leaders of the pack? Perhaps they're destined to remain focused as price-conscious, mostly copycat alternatives to branded products.

What role should strategy play in solving retail problems?

Strategy should be king for retailers when it comes to their private brands, but many still seem to struggle with that – it feels like it's mostly tactically-led. Surely it's better to have a long-term strategic approach to your business, understand the categories you want to operate in and your competition (whether branded or own label), and identify consumer needs, insights, purchase habits, and trends? This enables you to provide a relevant and differentiated brand offer. Without that, it's pretty tough to have a clear idea of how to move your brand forward.

What are the most common mistake retailers make with their brands?

Retailers need to leverage their bricks and mortar environments to offer consumers an experience that they can't get when ordering products online. They have the physical spaces and the ability to provide actual human contact, but they're just not thinking about how to use that to their advantage. What are currently giant warehouses of products need to become experiential showrooms. Think cooking classes using private brand products.

What advice do you have for retailers trying to take their brands to the next level?

Learn from branded products and think creatively about how to market their brands beyond the point of purchase. It doesn't have to cost a fortune. For example, Marks & Spencer recently relaunched Formula, its private label signature skincare range, with a new formulation, brand positioning and packaging design. It supported this relaunch by asking key beauty bloggers/influencers to review the products, and those positive reviews led to products flying off the shelves.

What will private brands look like 10 years from now?

For those private brands that position themselves mostly around (lower) price, perhaps we will see a movement towards completely stripping out graphic and structural packaging to drive down costs even further. Why need a label? Why need the bulky structure? Not only will this reduce costs, but it's more sustainable, more responsible, and more conscious.

Then there are the private brands that might decide to leverage all those insights collected by the retailer to really drive innovation. We might even begin to see a total reversal of the current state of play, where branded products imitate private label by creating their own cost-conscious product ranges. Some are already doing this, like Deciem's The Ordinary range of skincare treatments whose positioning is "to raise pricing and communication integrity in skincare."

STEVEN COX

Creative Director, Daymon
Connecticut, USA

Over the last year Amazon, Whole Foods, Lidl, and Jet have made aggressive moves into private brand, what impact are you seeing them have on your private brand clients and their brands?

Private brands are used to being the "underdog" to national brands but to go up against giants, like Amazon, can be a daunting task for almost any retailer. Our clients are looking to be more proactive and they understand the landscape is changing. We work with them to continually evolve and stay relevant in connecting to their targeted customers.

Retail disruptors, like Lidl and Jet, are either targeting a specific shopper or leveraging data to tailor a shopper's unique experience. While either may be difficult for smaller retailers, they can tailor solutions that are specific to their shoppers and the store environment to evolve their private brands.

What role should strategy play in solving retail problems?

Strategy should be at the forefront of all problem-solving discussion. Retailers often build a strategic plan every few years and then it easily gets pushed to the back burner. If you're able to continually make long-term strategic decisions, you will be able to proactively better your business for the long haul instead of continually putting out fires reactively.

Having a strategy means you are proactively building YOUR unique brand and YOUR experience, rather than reacting to what other competitors are doing. Retailers might ask the "Who?" and the "What?," but when you take strategy one step further, you must answer the meaningful "Why?"

What are the most common mistake retailers make with their brands?

A store's private brand program crosses all categories and lifestyles which requires flexibility. Five possible missteps include:

- Retailers often develop systems that are too rigid and don't allow for their products to compete within different categories.

- There are also often too many decision makers, each with their own vision of what the brand should be.

- There is a focus on execution before concept. Initial planning and strategy from concept to shelf is critical.

- Retailers may build brands based on what they (as decision makers) would want or what competitors are doing, not what their customers want.

- Retailers must educate shoppers on the brand's benefits, differentiation, or value proposition. Retailers often don't give their Private Brands enough marketing attention, and when they do, it is focused on products, not brand value.

What advice do you have for retailers trying to take their brands to the next level?

Know what your brands should stand for and, if you don't, shoppers will notice. Savvy consumers have an eye for detail and they want transparency. Retailers must be prepared to evolve as the landscape never sits still. Consumer trends, National Brand redesigns, Government Regulations or new Competitive Products have the propensity to impact the market and the success of a program depends on your ability to adapt. With leadership support, strategic goals, unique qualities and comprehensive marketing campaigns, your Private Brands will thrive.

What will private brands look like 10 years from now?

Private Brands will be leading National Brands while they continue to grow their presence on shelf. They offer the ability to provide unique solutions, not just "me too" versions of National Brands. By developing Private Brands' personalities and emotional connections with shoppers, they will be driving factors for loyalty in the growing competitive retail space.

LOE LIMPENS

Managing Partner, Yellow Dress Retail
The Netherlands

Over the last year Amazon, Whole Foods, Lidl, and Jet have made aggressive moves into private brand, what impact are you seeing them have on your private brand clients and their brands?

The near future will hold a 50 /50 balance between national brands and private brands, so everybody moving into this space will want to take a piece of the pie. In addition to this, the non-brick retailers moving into conventional brick & mortar retail space, will force brick & mortar to re-evaluate their business model, as their margins for home delivery are a lot lower than their online competitors. They will have to reduce the number of shops drastically and focus on home delivery logistics.

What role should strategy play in solving retail problems?

It is a key topic. In the fast moving and changing environment, you can only foresee the near future, if you know your products, the market, your competitors, etc. and based on this define your own role, eg. Strategy.

What are the most common mistake retailers make with their brands?

Retailers who put a product on shelf without a clear proposition (eg. better price, better quality, special variant, etc.) and anyway hope it will sell. On shelf is where the job starts, how to deliver the (private brand) message/promise to the customer.

What advice do you have for retailers trying to take their brands to the next level?

Private brands, should be the formula 1 of your store, speed to market is a key success factor. This is only possible when you use specialists, both internally and externally, on all levels.

What will private brands look like 10 years from now?

They will be divided into real and virtual brands. The retailer will use both to play it's online/offline platform, differentiating it's private brands from national brands.

PAULA BUNNY

Creative Director, Brother Design
New Zealand

Over the last year Amazon, Whole Foods, Lidl, and Jet have made aggressive moves into private brand, what impact are you seeing them have on your private brand clients and their brands?

As a New Zealand-based business, none of these brands feature in our market. However, there's been a lot of noise about Amazon opening across the ditch (in Australia) and the effect it may have on our retailers–online and off. After a few delays, it has finally opened its (virtual) doors, and the overwhelming reaction has been disappointment: pricing was pretty much on par or above what Australian consumers are used to, and private label isn't a big part of the Amazon Australia experience (yet).

There are plenty of rumors about Lidl joining their compatriot competitors Aldi in Australia, and fellow Schwarz group retailer Kaufland is opening, but nothing is definite. Meanwhile, Aldi continues to grow at 10% a year and their private label products feature strongly in Nielsen Australia's Product of the Year Awards. But on this side of the Tasman, it's still a two-horse race in supermarket retailing: Australia's Progressive group and New Zealand's own Foodstuffs.

What role should strategy play in solving retail problems?

Strategy is essential to solving problems in any aspect of business, including retail. Strategy is your compass, your Bible and the consultant at your shoulder. It provides you with a constant touchstone for decision-making. If it's not on strategy, it's not on.

But however beautiful the strategy, one should occasionally look at the results. I'd add that a beautiful strategy is never enough. The execution must be beautiful too. So beautiful that consumers simply cannot resist buying, and telling their friends. And a large part of that is the job of design.

What are the most common mistake retailers make with their brands?

In my experience, it's underinvestment. Too many retailers view private label as a cash cow, trying to extract margin at the expense of appeal. It has led to dull, unattractive quasi-brands that sell only on price to the bottom of the market. It's a recipe for stagnation at best, more likely long-term decline and failure.

What advice do you have for retailers trying to take their brands to the next level?

Do the opposite of the most common mistake: invest. And not just money, invest imagination. Private brands have all the same opportunities and scope as any brand, so use them. Investing thought and creativity into private brands will reap rich rewards.

What will private brands look like 10 years from now?

As retailers and marketers learn from the ongoing success of private brands, they'll be better able to replicate winning formulas and avoid mistakes. So I expect more and better private brands. And of course they'll be increasingly sold online.

Where I think there will be significant change is in the ways private brands use technology and digital networks as part of the brand experience. We're only seeing the tip of the iceberg in terms of private brands using social media, digital connections, tailoring the customer experience and loyalty. There's a long way to go, but the potential is immense.

JUDGES

Paco Adin
Creative Director
Supperstudio
Spain

Rick Barrack
Chief Creative Officer & Managing
Partner
CBX
New York, USA

Danielle Beal
Creative Director
The Creative Pack
California, USA

Paula Bunny
Creative Director
Brother Design
New Zealand

Linda Casey
Editor-in-chief
Brand Experience Magazine
Chicago, USA

Don Childs
SVP, Executive Creative Director
BrandImage
Ohio, USA

Maria Dubuc
President
MBD
Massachusetts, USA

Steven Cox
Creative Director
Daymon
Connecticut, USA

Charlene Codner
Founder & Chief Creative Officer
Fish out of Water Design
Ontario, Canada

Michael Duffy
Group Creative Director & Partner
Equator Design
Illinois, USA

Masanori Eto
Creative Director
AdBrain, Inc.
Tokyo, Japan

John Kalkowski
Editor in Chief
BRANDPackaging Magazine
Illinois, USA

Loe Limpens
Managing Partner
Yellow Dress Retail
Netherlands

Fred Richards
CCO & Partner
Kaleidoscope
Illinois, USA

Nick Vaus
Partner & Creative Director
DewGibbons + Partners
United Kingdom

Senior Package Designer
Creative Director, MBD
Massachusetts, USA

ZHOU Wenjun
Founder, Creative Director &
Architect
524 Studio
China

CHRISTOPHER DURHAM

Co-founder, the Vertex Awards
President, My Private Brand
CHARLOTTE, NORTH CAROLINA

MY [PRIVATE] BRAND.

My Private Brand was launched by Christopher Durham in late 2008 and has quickly become the most widely read daily publication on Private Brands in the world. It's the leading resource for retailer owned Brand development, analysis, best practices, news, information and jobs. With readership from retailers, private brand manufacturers, branding agencies and thought leaders from around the world, My Private Brand is designed to foster innovation, encourage debate and write the next chapter of brand management—Private Brand Management.

Christopher Durham is a world-renowned private brand consultant, author, and retailer who built million-dollar brands for global supermarket retailer Delhaize and led strategy and brand development for Lowe's Home Improvement's $18 billion private brand portfolio. He is the founder of the groundbreaking private brand website My Private Brand and the co-founder of the international private brand package design competition The Vertex Awards. In 2017 he introduced Velocity: The My Private Brand Conference a thought leadership gathering of private brand executives focused on creating the future or retail owned brands.

He has consulted with retailers around the world on their private brand portfolios including Ahold, Family Dollar, Petco, Staples, Office Depot, Best Buy, Metro (Canada), TLW (Taiwan) REI and Hola (Taiwan).

Durham has published six definitive books on private brands, including his first book, Fifty2: The My Private Brand Project and his newest book, Vanguard: Vintage Originals, a visual tour of innovation, disruption and design in private brand dating back to the mid-1800's.

Dynamic in his presentation while down to earth and frank in his opinions, he has presented at numerous conferences, including FUSE, The Dieline Conference, Packaging that Sells, Omnishopper and PLMA'a annual trade show in Chicago and Amsterdam.

PHILLIP RUSSO

Co-founder, the Vertex Awards
Founder/Publisher/Editor, Global Retail Brands
NEW YORK, NEW YORK

Global Retail Brands

Global Retail Brands magazine was launched to promote the best examples of retail brand marketing from around the world. Industry experts from all facets of private label contribute to the magazine, providing an unbiased, international voice of authority. Its design departs from the norm to reflect the industry's creativity.

Phillip is the Founder/Publisher/Editor of Global Retail Brands magazine and a 18-year veteran of the private label industry. He was responsible for Private Label magazine's global expansion and return to profitability prior to the successful launch of Global Retail Brands.

His appreciation for design and its successful application is rooted in the design field, where he headed a trade publishing division which produced trade shows, magazines and digital for the commercial interior design industry. Before Private Label, he was publisher of the modern design/lifestyle magazine, DWELL, one of the most successful magazine launches of its time.

He is the principal of Kent Media, based in New York City, which publishes Global Retail Brands and a number of Design Show directories.

THANK
YOU

TO OUR SPONSORS WHO GRACIOUSLY SUPPORT THE VERTEX AWARDS

elmwood

ELMWOOD.COM

MBD.

MBDESIGN.COM

teri

TERISTUDIOS.COM

VOCCII

VOCCII.COM

www.ingramcontent.com/pod-product-compliance
Lightning Source LLC
Chambersburg PA
CBHW041545260326
41914CB00016B/1558